Things I Wish I'd Said
To Winifred

By Doctor Paul Barker

September 2015

ISBN Number

ISBN #: ISBN 978-1-329-71410-6

Copyright Dr Paul Barker 2015

For Jack Tom and Soph

Things I Wish I'd Said to Winifred

Contents

All Things Pass

Salt-caked fingers form sand-scoured shambles,
Pointing, tide-tossed, to an iron sky.
Unheeded runes, lone companions for the ceaseless wind's
carol,
Whisper '*all things must pass*'.
But
Even the bellowing bass counterpoint,
In rock defeated caverns, is heard only by those borne of air,
'*All things must change*', they say,
But
Wind -harrowed, their words composed of air, return to air
unheard.

Things I Wish I'd Said to Winifred

I adore the rusty deceit of your eyes,
That mock my years with kindness.
That I may never know your first electric kiss,
Or hear the sibilant sigh of silk on secret floors,
Or cup your Sadness in my hands,
And breathe its embers into warmth.
Lions roamed your dreams, cloaked in misty savannah
spices,
Now bottled and dulled by the years of separation, they lose
their vital musk.
And you muse that nobody will listen anymore.

An evening on Robinswood Farm

Which golden hand then, coddles the corn,
And plumps the barley head?
That cups the hazel in hoary hand?
How many, have stopped here and wondered,
At your changing face?

Time stalks these hills and touches with love,
The rusted harrow wheel, skulking in the hedgerow,
And muses, perhaps a little sadly, of gentler times,
And paints my face –and yours- with silver web.

On the 3am Cockerel

A ludicrous fowl is the cockerel,
As he pivots and gestures and crows!
But I hate most of all, his 3 am call,
It's the way he was made I suppose.

A ludicrous fowl is the cockerel,
All fiddling feathers and comb!
Just why was he made with such jaunty brocade?
Like a second rate General from Rome!

A ludicrous fowl is the cockerel,
As he struts round the yard like a swell!
But the best place for cocks is inside a fox,
And you can keep all the others as well!!

Cliffs of Moonlight

Cliffs of moonlight tranced the sky, below a blasted moor, and silver-
green the casement by, an ancient Oaken door.
A cruel body, midnight cloaked, he stood foursquare and proud,
A shuttered lantern guttered, choked, wore darkness as its shroud.

The sea below a blackened tongue- caressing jagged teeth,
A heartless shore with coast unsung, and roaring caves beneath.
He moved like velvet falling, to the cliff tops severed edge,
And spied a Shallop calling, with a single moonlit pledge,

He hailed unto the spritsail rig, a graveyard glimmer light,
For a Barquentine - a Spanish Brig- would be their prize tonight.
A broad-reach to the North and East, the Shallop's rigging cried,
As broiling coal-black waters breach, the gunwales rode the tide.

And ranged along the foreshore, holding midnight in their hand,
Witnessed only by the winds roar, on that lonely, ancient strand.
A band of Cornish blaggards, with the devil in their eyes,
Waited hungry worn and haggard, for the Balearic prize.

Atop the cliff, a pistol's bark rent the troubled night,
And to a man the shuttered dark, erupted into light.
And blown athwart that fickle sea, the Spaniard hove to shore,
The shallop drifted in her lee, like a sailor to his whore.

And tenderly she led the way, the Shallop to the Barque,
A Spanish flagship led astray, false harbour through the dark.
All in a moment lost at sea, the Shallop's mast-light failed,
The Barque she made time steadily, and into false-lights sailed.

The keelson firstly struck the bar, an ecstasy of tortured night,
A livid jagged blackened scar, her belly rent, defined her plight.
She sat there broken in the surf, a mournful carol joined the waves,
The Wreckers plundered all her worth and sent her crew to watery graves.

And often on the palest night, where cliffs of moonlight trance the sky,
He knows to find a fearful sight that stirs behind his coal-black eye.
For sailing clad in midnight, and hard by to the shore.,
A ghostly crew show false-lights, up to the Oaken door.

And stumbling -a man possessed- with midnight in his hand,
He signals once -and finds his rest- upon the salt-black sand.
And ever more on stormy nights, below the blasted moor,
A ghost ship setting false lights, tempts wreckers to the shore.

The Pumpkin Tree and the Whispering Tree

Night-clad at my window, when dark enchants the sky,
And misty looping ribbons dance to whispers by and by,
The Pumpkin tree stands listening. Dark fingers pierce the sky,
Whilst the whispering tree sighs gently, you can hear her if you try.
She sings of tiny acorns that grow up to be ships,
And boys that climb and girls that scold the boys with cherry lips,
For all good children understand they never should have played,
Near the midnight forest, or into the moonlight strayed.
And she sings of pirate treasures, in chests of finest Oak,
Whilst the pumpkin tree listens silently beneath a midnight cloak.

The pumpkin tree was once a child, who tarried for too long,
And strayed too near the whispering tree enchanted by her song.
For those that stop to listen, succumbing to her charms,
When the old moon slumbers gently safe in the new moons arms,
Will become part of the forest and it's rumoured on the breeze.
That their tiny faces are etched within the bark of midnight trees.
Night-clad at my window, when dark enchants the sky,
And misty looping ribbons dance to whispers by and by.
The Pumpkin tree stands listening, dark fingers pierce the sky,
The whispering tree sighs gently, you can hear her if you try.

A treasury for children, a Victorian ghost story

The moon bathed in a silver pond, as night time closed the day,
And Mother whispers Vespers as we settle down to pray,
'Thank you for the friendly dark' we faithfully intone,
And father ushers in the moon as we were left alone.

And peeping through my fingers, as the whispers fill my head,
A 'Treasury for Children' lying open by my bed,
'There's something of the midnight', father's words of admonition,
But never underestimate the allure of prohibition.

For reading by the moonlight when the pictures play and dance,
And coal black eyes of fairy-folk ensnare us in their trance.
Trapped within the brushwork of the artist's patient hand,
A tiny frightened face peers back from some otherworldly land.

Standing in her simple shift and tiny painted shawl,
Sometimes in every picture and sometimes not at all,
Perhaps a single twist of smoke from a witch's cottage range,
Or staring from the window of a lonely moated grange.

And as we grew so she would too, upon the painted page,
The girl became a woman though she never seemed to age.
One night she simply disappeared as we left the nursery,
And we never saw that girl again but prayed that she was free.

The Owls parliament

In times now long forgotten and so as not to start an argument,
An owlish convocation formed and deemed themselves a
'Parliament'.
They met deep in a forest where the churlish daylight frowns,
And for each and every animal agreed collective nouns.
They started with their cousin birds and some were quite absurd,
Swans lent themselves to 'symphony' but ended up a 'herd'!
For starlings, 'murmeration' because they sound just like they're
yelling,
For crows it was a 'murder' and for ravens, 'storytelling'.
A 'gaggle' of geese when on the ground, a 'skein' whilst on the wing,
A 'scold' of jays, a 'flock' of gulls and here's a funny thing,
You see the peacock was a problem for the owlish convocation,
And after many days of arguing they agreed on 'ostentation'.
Now drunk with self importance, they essayed a vote of thanks,
Before turning their attention to other taxonomic ranks.
So the tiger became an 'ambush' and the bears became a 'sleuth',
And zebra's were a 'zeal' but only when they're on the hoof.
There was a 'bloat' of hippopotami, a 'mob' of kangaroos,
And the oddest one of all was an 'implausibility' of gnus.
For cats it was a 'nuisance' whereas for dogs it was a 'pack'.
For swine it was a 'sounder' and for jellyfish a 'smack'.
A 'leap' of leopards alliterates as does a 'lounge´ of lizards,
An 'aurora' for the Polar bears whose fur was made from blizzards,
The Parliament discussed mankind, and because they ran around
apace,
Without a thought for other animals they'd be called the 'human
race'.

Clearly confused by oxymora

The 'pain for pleasure principle' is 'disgustingly delicious',
Whilst 'passively aggressive' seems both trite and injudicious,
It's said by fools 'anarchy rules' and so's the 'sound of silence',
Whilst 'civil war' and 'friendly fire' are for those disposed to
violence.
A 'little pain has never hurt' when speaking of 'ill health',
Or 'I'm deeply superficial' said Andy Warhol of himself.
There's 'sweet sorrow' and 'O loving hate' for when Romeo's in
trouble,
And 'faith unfaithful kept him falsely true' scores Tennyson the
double.
Politician's muse and chew 'old news', they 'agree to disagree',,
So thank goodness for the 'peacekeeper bomb' to keep the country
free!
'Cruel to be kind' and 'solid air' exemplify the 'soft rock' song,
And one that's queer is 'Final frontier' which is semantically wrong.
An 'eloquent silence' - it may be said- describes a simple kiss,
And memories are 'bittersweet' when we stop to reminisce.
The chances that there's life on Mars are 'astronomically small',
And it's no surprise the 'devout atheist' denies that there is a God at
all.
We may say 'pretty ugly' or 'terribly good', but on one thing I've
never been surer,
The list we've perused leaves me 'clearly confused' about how to use
oxymora!

An affair beginning to end

Slumbering sighing,
Gently caressing,
Loving you freely,
Never possessing.
Infatuation,
Blistering, burning,
Stifling marriage,
Chasming yearning.
Heart stopping moments
Tasting your soul,
Words that are empty,
Love on parole.
Moody and hungry,
Scanning your eyes,
Obsessing and scheming,
Drowning in lies.
Dying by inches,
Cloyingly greedy,
You become colder,
I become needy.
Visceral aching,
Guilt to atone,
Dissatisfaction,
A love from the bone

Couplets on your ego

Your attempts at seeking happiness put the horse before the carriage,
You look to find contentment as an add-on to a marriage.
You know Latin, Greek and Portuguese, but speak no common sense,
Self -delusion is your common tongue and drink your recompense
You seek wisdom through the Coptic scripts and chanting ululations,
But the search goes on for inner peace through external validations.
You're a chaos of cathectic drives, a creation of the id,
For the god you serve has appetites religious views forbid.

You're funny, fey and pithy with a superficial charm,
But social isolation is your weapon of self-harm.
You believe in natural justice and you put your faith in karma,
Whilst everyone's a walk on part in your psychodrama.
Your ego is a Trojan horse that could breach a city wall,
Just remember what I told you, pride may come before a fall.

on your death when I was a child:
An Etheree

As
You left
You promised
That you would try
To let me know that
You were a breath away
And I listened so hard that
I heard only the sea in shells
A lifetime later I realise that
There never was so perfect a silence.

Memories of an Irish Funeral (When I was very young)

Michael Tyers died, aged seven
'Resting here in sweet repose.'
Did they send your shade to heaven
As your corporeal froze?
Father Joseph sweetly stumbled
To eulogize for one so small.
And in the Latin gently mumbled,
How you bore no sin at all.
But come the Glorious Resurrection,
Reunited you would be.
Take refuge in the Lord's protection
Sleeping with Christ's family.
But your mother broken-hearted
To bid farewell to one so small.
To leave you with the dear departed
wrapped simply in your funerary pall.
She stayed late into the evening
Lit a grave light at your head,
To satiate herself with grieving,
Wishing she was freshly dead.
And your father lately married
Drank himself into a swoon.
And at the graveside never tarried
Knowing he must join you soon.

Sweeny Todd Demon Barber of Fleet Street (A song)

Candy cane striping, totem of your art,
A terrible hunger consuming your heart.
Dark back street squalor a Starling's wing night,
With soot crusted windows that torture the light,
Smog dancing zephyrs that skulk in the fog,
The back-drop to Fleet Street's most heinous prologue.

Benjamin Barker a barber most rare,
Brought 'Skill and attention' to each head of hair,
Deported for crimes that Judge Turpin alleges,
Retuning to London with barbarous pledges,
A tonsorial parlour atop river Fleet,
Providing a source of the rarest red meat.

Through shambling London to a Soho estate,
The judge and his young ward bemoaning her fate,
Wedded to Turpin through venal cupidity,
And singly appalled by the ermine's rancidity,
A victim of avarice and deeds that were darker,
And jealously guarded was Joanna Barker.

With a schisming ego that most would find odd,
The demon of Fleet Street is one 'Sweeny Todd',
Driven to madness by the loss of his daughter,
And treating his clients like lambs to the slaughter,
Seeking salvation through actions depraved,
Sending souls to their maker pomaded and shaved!

Below in the pie shop the corpse thinly sliced,
Then thrice through the mincer and liberally spiced,
Entombed then in pastry and served golden brown,
Pies full of body, the finest in town!
A special arrangement with the parlour above it,
And front of the house the mob-hatted Nell Lovett.

The end of this story's a grizzly affair,
When Turpin asked Todd to attend to his hair,
The witnesses spoke of an awful affray,
And later three bodies were carried away,
Now only in death did he find recognition,
Todd took his own life in an act of contrition.

The Legend of Tristan and Isolde

part 1:-

About a stones cast from the keep, a tiny Bethel cowed with age,
The moted silence brooding deep, a liturgy to Tristan's rage.
He carried darkness in his heart and pensive sadness was his name,
Queen Blancheflor a soul apart, King Rivalin his father -Thane.

A courtly noble true and fair, his Blazon flamed with red and gold,
Like snow in spring his flaxen hair and strangest myths the fates foretold.
To Mark he was a very son and skilled of hand at hunt and lyre,
Of kinsmen but a single one named Gouvernail his brother-squire.

He knelt before the Jesse Screen, as shafting moonlight closed the day,
And swore an oath to find his Queen and death befall the Irish Fey.
A Celtic giant sung by bards with flint-black eye and hair aflame,
Envenomed were his arrow shards and Morholt was his given name.

Christian ranks of Wessex bold, gave voice before the Pagan foe,
Until their blood was frozen cold and wasted on the crimson snow.
The fury burned in Tristan's breast as ranks of Bonnacht's met their doom,
For three long nights he took no rest, pale death before a russet moon.

Through the furious battle close, Sir Tristan spied the shock-haired gall,
But death had dealt an equal dose and King Mark's flag looked sure to fall.
A battle anthem split the night, well met upon that butchered field.
And shook the earth with mythic might, where shield met sword and sword cleft shield.

Upon the coming of the day, the slain were numbered two and two,
And Tristan kissed his sword to pray, as Morholt's blood was frozen through,
But wounded by the blighted brand, Sir Tristan fell 'cross Morholt's shade,
A bane no mortal could withstand, his gemmy eyes began to fade.

Embowered in a woodbine glade, a melancholy seized his heart,
And all about the woods they prayed, for Tristan's shade safe to depart.
But Tristan mused to tell his squire, 'an aged crone of magic deep',
Her skills well known across the shire, for life and deathly secrets keep.

She bound his wounds full tenderly and gently kissed his noble brow,
She knew not what the curse may be. But well discerned the where and how,
'Isolode child of Anguish King', would lift the curse came Beldam's call,
'And love' said she - the only thing- that Adam found before his fall.

Part 2:-

And by and by the coast awhile, a barge and oarsmen rode the tides,
Hibernia the magic isle, to fortress where King Anguish bides.
Sir Tristan and his brother-squire voyaged beneath a troubled sky,

His fevered wounds were tongues of fire, his dreams the hope in Charon's eye.

The Irish Sea was stormy black and fickle winds confound the way,
The jewelled Welkin marked their track, and tortured dreams seduced the day,
A face with verdant eyes aflame and auburn hair that flowed blood-red.
A Celtic goddess none could tame; a golden circlet crowned her head.

She gazed upon his face perchance, to find a secret lovers sign,
But in that glassy countenance she well perceived a love divine,
And stooping, touched his temple fair, and kissed his silent frozen brow,
Reciting then a Celtic prayer, she bound their hands with lovers vow.

And summoned by Isolde's lips, Sir Tristan woke from darkest sleep,
A love that no words could eclipse. So rare that all the passions keep,
And though they shared no common tongue, their eyes bespoke a thousand words,
That they may stay forever young and fly as freely as the birds.

They lay entwined in lovers rest but Tristan's thoughts were brooding dark,
King Anguish words must soon attest, Isolde promised to King Mark.
Sir Tristan ever loyal, true, had sworn a blood-oath to his liege.
His perfect love he must eschew, his heart forever under siege.

Part 3:-

They journeyed back with darkest heart, to Cornwall's lonely blasted shore,
Her maid well steeped in blackest art, pledged her oath and this she swore,
That if in life they may not love, then death unite them evermore,
But could not make them drink thereof, for brave sir Tristan she'd adore.

And sometime on that moonlit night, Brangwain formed the secret brew,
But not the draught of deadly blight; a potion to ensnare the two.
And drank they deeply of the cup, that yearning passions overcame,
The instant they had taken sup, a perfect love two souls aflame.

And from the cliffs they spied the barque which carried midnight in its sail,
He rode to greet them good King Mark, and watched them silent at the rail,
Brave Sir Knight full in his armour, bewitched him with her peerless grace,
Enthralled by her Queenly glamour, entranced by her beauteous face.

And on that lonely blasted strand, where soughing winds bemoaned their fate,
King Mark's men were close at hand and Stole Isolde to Mark's estate.
Sir Tristan's heart was broke in two, so cruelly parted from his love,
And though a loyal Knight and true, he trembled like a wounded dove.

Though she married good King Mark, he never owned her truest heart,
And from her tower gray and stark, she'd watch the deer and wild bird dart,
And flit into the forest clear. And each dark day she'd sit and wait,

For shadows of her love appear, a voice perchance, a creaking gate.

She never saw her love again; he dwelt forever in her breast,
And Tristan crippled by the pain, died alone, his heart bereft,
But Brangwain knew her lady's heart, and watched her vital beauty pall,
And made a sup so both depart, in death not life love conquers All.

Cluedo

An old country retreat just for setting the scene,
Where our characters meet and the Reverend Green,
With a length of old rope in the billiard room,
Dreams of plans to elope with Miss Scarlet and soon,
They'd start up a bureau and become private eyes,
Employ Hercule Poirot, and out of work spies,
Like Ironside and Sam Spade, and Quincey MD,
So the Reverend prayed for an angel or Three.
To help solve the murder (by a slash to the throat),
Of the infamous author of (Murder she wrote),
Then all would join forces with the canny old priest,
It was horses for courses for Hopkirk (deceased),
So they met in the cellar where the corpse lay a cooling,
To assemble the facts, whilst the blood was a pooling,
There was a length of old rope and a severed metacarpal,
Which was low hanging fruit to amazing Jane Marple,
There were early wins for the Thompson twins,
Deducing how the *corpus delicti* had died,
On the twist of rope was an envelope with three little cards inside,
'Miss Scarlet with a bloodied knife and in the ballroom too',
Of his plan to elope there'd be no hope if all the cards spoke true,
'Oh hell NO' cried the errant vicar and whipped a pistol from his knicker.
Miss Scarlet made a move to grab it, so he pulled another from his habit,
And BANG BANG BANG he shot them DEAD,
And fired the last round through his head.
So game players although it may look like fun it,
Doesn't pay to meddle in another's whodunit!

Crossword Competition

'Have you got two down my dear?'
I think it's *'Colposinquanonia'*, estimating beauty by the size
of the breast.
What of 'one who leers my love?'
Simply *'gymnophoria'*, the erudite sensation of being
mentally undressed.

What of three across my queen?
I think that it's *'jentacular'* pertaining to one's breakfast at
the beginning of the day.
'C' something *'N'* my love?
That one is *'concillabule'*, a meeting of two people but in a
clandestine way.

Who'd of thought of *'qualtagh'* sweet?
As I recall you did my love. 'The first person that you see
after vacating of your house'.
And did you get ten down my prince?
'Alphamegamia', The wedlock of a younger bride to a much
much older spouse.

'Thirteen letters, Greenland song?'
Yes that was *'Mallemarocking'*, the carousing of a sailor
aboard a Greenland ship,
And who'd of known 14 across?
Now that was *'Callipygean'* to thrill to well-turned buttocks,
and a liking for the hip.

Twelve letters, starts with 'C' my love?
That's simply *'cruciverbalist'*, when completion of a
crossword becomes one's favoured chore,
And I believe you've found the prizeword sweet?
Yes, I think that it was *'aeolist'* the pretense of inspiration in
an unreconstructed bore.

On the coming of the Doctor

Veiled mists of shadow play, glimpses of you,
Through the cataract of time.
Though fractured words have burned away,
You live within me still, carried like a traveller's ember.
Even now you cling to me, gaunt, pinched,
A child's face with frightened eyes,
A cruel prison of a body to which sleep is but a distant
shore,
Shriven by an agony of spirit, taut with fear, the one
sacrament that we two may share,
Until,
Sleep comes, falling ever further,
We two, entwined within the heady reek of morphoea,
Without hope of change,
Falling further,
Still now.
Doll like,
I breathe the pilgrim in you into the next adventure.

Springs Heartbeat

Spring's
Heart beat.
Systolic
Flutterings.
A quickening
Forces tiny blanching fingers into earthen pockets
Nurtured by a juvenile sun
Introspective, fickle
Single parent.
Cupped in the hands of a dying winter.
Frigid breath
Whispers 'Change'
Until glutted upon their mother's colostrum
As one.
They emerge,
Through the earth,
Through rock walls.
To dance in an ephemeral instant
For the swelling sun.
Spring's
Heartbeat.

The Man with the Old Tin Roof

Once upon a time there was a man who lived in a place where the skies were huge. Sometimes the sun shone and sometimes there were big sad storms. More often, the sky was gray and dull. Because you see, the whole sky was sad when he was sad and when he was happy, brilliant sunshine lit the days. He lived in a tiny house with an old tin roof. At night, when the wind sighed in the long pampas, he cried because you see, he was utterly alone. One day he met a woman who was beautiful. He loved her with all his heart. She brought with her, her Father. He was a farmer and a wise old man. He taught the man in the tin house to sow seeds and tend the fields. The old man watched and chuckled as the younger man tried to learn. He was patient and kind and became a father to the man with the old tin roof. Soon the farm was beautiful and the three of them lived together so happily. And do you know what's more? If you close your eyes really tightly, you can see the tiny house in the swaying pampas and see the man and woman and the old farmer sitting on the storm porch. But I will bet that when you see the huge skies they are now filled with sunshine. And though the man in the old tin house grew old, he never ever felt alone again.

Polypharmacy Mantra

Now there's 20,000 different pills , in the BNF today,
A pill for curing every ill, Or so the papers say!
For some can make you poo some more, whilst others water pass,
You can them subcutaneously IV or up the ass!

Now a hospice is the perfect place, for sanctuary and peace.
To bring a smile back to the face, a space where worries cease.
So when a person enters in and with compassion fills,
There's just one chance to get it right by checking all their pills!

Give thought then to the renal tract, a mantra we all sing .
The science though is inexact but here's a funny thing.
By checking now for AKI can keep our patient's swell,
Think stopping NSAID's, water pills ACE inhibitors as well.

We start with metoclopramide for keeping supper down.
And add a little sertraline for them that's prone to frown.
So many pills and potions, it's time to stop and think.
Are they really needed or should we wash them down the sink!!!

And then we treat for side effects, with yet more pill and potion
'your problems' really quite complex', well here's a crazy notion.
'Beneficence' a concept which should teach us all discretion,
And stop us simply practicing biochemical obsession.

Reducing polypharmacy, the order of the day,
Firstly do no harm you see, the Hippocrotean way.
Reduce then by a quarter, or even by a half,
And thank you all for listening I hope we made you laugh.

On NHS Managers

On *'April one'*, should be the 'first of April',

Let's bring some *'branding'* to the table,

Our *'bandwidth'* is just a little too tight,

They've *'shifted goalposts'* over night,

And strictly between me and you,

They've refused the *'global overview'*

So, now please give a *'ballpark figure'*,

And 'drill-down' to what we might deliver,

Or take the *'helicopter view'*,

And think our way *'through skies of blue'*

'Let's find a table to bring it to',

Or *'run it up a flagpole'*, where,

Eager hands salute thin air,

With not a mention of doc or nurses;

An edifice to risk averseness,

Or let's *'throw some context around'*,

(Think I just heard ultrasound!!),

'*There's no I in team'*, I think it wise,

'*To see if we can't incentivise'*,

And understand the guidelines (NICE)!

With '*client-focused, critical missions'*,

Now something about long-term conditions,

Let's talk about patients I hear you shout,

'*let's graze the cows in the ideas field and see exactly what drops out'*

With '*providers, commissioners, the old new contract'*,

And '*single points of bloody contact'*

Today I've watched you '*bottom out'*,

And '*sweat your asset'*, and throughout

This meeting you've been a lexical joke,

Probably '*pushing some metaphorical envelope'*,

I really don't want to '*catch the lingo'*

And that was HOUSE in management bingo.

An ode to my cold sore

A blitzkrieg march in shortest order,
Redefining my vermillion border.

Charlie

Livid bruising amber skies,
Cross umber fields of trodden chalk,
Soft bones of hillside, feet baptize,
Fading, where we two would walk.

And shingle sighs as sea laments,
Upon a final blasted shore,
And turning once you fade from sense,
To own your evermore.

Autumn's remembrance

Pleated deep brown baritones of death Gray earth,
A stirring. Clot red leaves dance to the musing of a careless
wind ,
Cajoling the dying year through a cataract of mist.
I remember you dancing, parting the mists like a shroud.
Welcoming the Autumn with her glutted womb.
And I mused, perhaps a little sadly, how love, like the year
had flown.

Sunday Afternoon Truths

A slick afternoon, sepia-toned and ageing,
You stand distant and cold like a breathing postcard,
I have no words to paint you,
No heart to beat in time with you,
I feel nothing. Empty, corrupted and broken,
Like dust in forgotten rooms; lazy, once vital,
Love lays dying, without hope for change.

Remember the sun setting in her eyes?
Remember the last open-sore breath,
Reeking across my shoulder?
The miasma of corruption,
And through all of this you spoke to me,
Softly, without words, the gentle sighs of souls touching,
A visceral understanding. Gut-felt.

And now I see you through a mirror,
Never, really comprehending,
The agony of your soul.
Our speech, tortured upon a rack of broken words,
Love confessed of pain.
And yet, to you it means so much.
To me, dried and barren, fetid with age.

Then, as the afternoon gasps into evening,
There comes a whisper, a confession of love lost,
And congealed regret.
Stifled and dying yet sharp-edged and cutting,
It speaks to the adventurer in me,
To run child-like, blindly searching,
For that which never could have been.